BOXELDER BUG
VARIATIONS

A MEDITATION ON AN IDEA
IN LANGUAGE AND MUSIC

BOXELDER BUG
VARIATIONS

A MEDITATION ON AN IDEA
IN LANGUAGE AND MUSIC

Bill Holm

"EVERY OBJECT RIGHTLY SEEN UNLOCKS A NEW FACULTY OF THE SOUL."
—SAMUEL TAYLOR COLERIDGE

MILKWEED EDITIONS

96 97 98 99 00   10 9 8 7 6

A LAKES AND PRAIRIES AWARD BOOK
Published by Milkweed Editions
430 First Avenue North, Suite 400
Minneapolis, Minnesota 55401
Books may be ordered from the above address

Designed and illuminated by R.W. Scholes © 1985
Edited by Emilie Buchwald
Music Script by Jim Phillips © 1985

Library of Congress Catalog Card Number: 85-61616
ISBN 0-915943-43-3

*This publication was supported in part by a grant
provided by the Metropolitan Council from funds
appropriated by the Minnesota State Legislature and
from funds raised by Metro Area Arts organizations
at the Minnesota Jam to preserve the Arts.*

Two of these poems have appeared, in slightly different form, in *The Gathering Post:*
"Poets and Scientists Find Boxelder Bugs Useful for Both Metaphor and Experiment,"
and "The Boxelder Bug Takes His Stand on the Pro-Life Issue and Its Roots in
Industrial Capitalism."

These bugs are dedicated to the Minneota friends who have for years sustained, loved, helped, and fed one another. No New Yorker or Bloomsburyite ever had a set so lovely. They gave me the bugs with their speech and their ideas. They are, as the phone book finds them: John Allen, Gary DeCramer, Daren Gislason, Tom Guttormsson, Maureen Ahern Johnson, Rollie Johnson, Gail Perrizo, and the ghosts in the house.

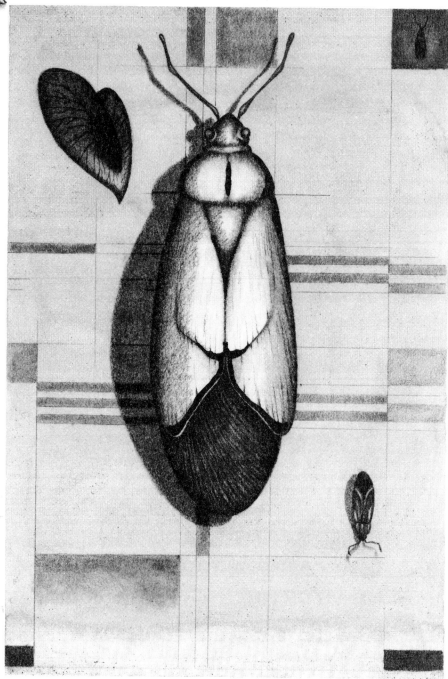

CONSIDER THE BOXELDER BUG

The bug's Latin name is several times as large as itself: *Leptocoris trivittatus*. Such grand dignity in those syllables! It ought to be a Roman emperor's name, or a phrase from a Requiem Mass, a choir of hooded monks singing the ancient tune in a stone cathedral flooded with incense, smoky light, and echoes. Try this: "Leptocoris, son of noble Trivittatus, went forth to Gaul with an hundred legions, laying waste all about him as he brought the barbarian under his heel with sword and shield and valorous deed." Or, try this:

Yet the bug at his full growth is hardly a half inch long and weighs less than a duck's pinfeather. Imagine him crawling along huge, carved stone letters on an emperor's tomb: LEPTOCORIS TRIVIT-TATUS, taking twenty minutes to find his way out of the O before mounting the bottom of the R.

Such persistence is one of the endearing qualities of the boxelder bug. In Minnesota, they are regarded with a kind of good-natured hatred tinged with grudging admiration for their tenacity in making their way into houses, and insistence on remaining alive once there. The boxelder bug lives symbiotically with the boxelder tree, eating and breeding without killing or starving the tree itself, a harmless, amiable, parasitic friendship.

In Virginia, I often puzzled friends by mentioning boxelder trees in poems and conversations. In pine, live oak, and magnolia country, you do not find boxelder. They are prairie trees, growing quick and vigorous on dry grassland where trees don't do well. They flourish where cornstalks and basketball players are the tallest flora on the horizon.

Even in Minnesota, the boxelder is a weed tree, a welcome windbreak in farm groves, but discouraged in towns and parks, and forbidden in elegant suburbs. The boxelder's disadvantages are con-

siderable: rapid and chaotic growth; an appearance gnarled, disorderly, and lacking in proportion; wood too soft and mushy to be useful for carving or lumber; a poor, fast-burning fireplace wood. Furthermore, it hatches boxelder bugs.

Their single advantage is, however, great; they grow enthusiastically where grander and more delicate trees refuse to take root. They are not very particular about water or sun, and tolerate both blizzards and scorching winds. They accept weather and do their business: grow, and provide bird homes and boxelder bug hatcheries. In a landscape with neither shade nor escape from wind, they are loved despite their ugliness by horses, owls, and most people.

On my father's farm north of Minneota, a few cottonwoods towered over the rest of the grove, dropping cotton on boxelders below them, their noisy leaves glittering all afternoon. But boxelders made up in number what they lacked in size; good pig yard trees, keeping hogs happy and cool on hot days. Having seen nothing else, I imagined northern Minnesota woods as endless miles of boxelders, the forest floor crawling with lively bugs. Pines and birches disappointed me when I finally saw them, shapes too regular, usual, straight; and they gave no boxelder bugs.

Like humans, the bug is aware that Minnesota is not the kind of place where one lives outdoors and unprotected in winter. Sensibly, he and an inexhaustible supply of his relatives make their way into your house each fall by means never adequately explained. There they set up winter encampments in window sills, inside light fixtures, in cupboards, in back of furniture, almost anywhere warm.

My boxelder bugs have odd preferences. They love radio dials, phonograph speakers, amplifiers, pianos, and harpsichords. Some would argue that this is because of the warmth and vibrations, but I prefer to think it is because of their taste for Bach and Vivaldi. And coffee! A coffee tin rattling and the first whistle of boiling water signal vigorous bug activity. They actually seem to hurry across the stove, waiting to be embalmed in grounds, scalded by water, or drowned in a Johnstown flood of finished steaming coffee. They seem to share their landlord's tastes; a desire to please is not unusual among boxelder bugs.

As insects go, they have a utilitarian and unpretentious look: small, flat, with six legs, the usual antennae, a dark brown, almost black thorax decorated with thin red veins in the shape of a peace symbol, none of the mosquito's wispy delicacy or the cockroach's armored malignity.

Indeed, they are peaceful bugs. Aside from existing in great numbers and wanting to keep you company, they have no unpleasant habits. They make no noise, move slowly, eat nothing of yours, are not poisonous, do not smell, do not bite, and live mostly in out-of-the-way places that you do not wish to use yourself. Good house guests, as insects go. They even die discreetly, simply drying up after blizzards start. In spring, you find their dusty hulls inside chandeliers or windowsills — a weightless dry parchment with the body evaporated out, a bit of residue at the bottom of a pan, an ash left from a crematorium, a flake of pepper.

Boxelder bugs are legendary in their ability to survive your vigorous efforts to kill them. They can be frozen, incinerated, poisoned, or crushed, and survive the ordeal far more calmly than their tormentors. They seem to have an inner metabolic clock that tells them when to dry up in a couch cushion, and until that alarm rings, they go on with their bugly lives, the Presbyterians of the insect kingdom, believing that the boxelder deity foreordained their lives and will not summon them out of turn. Their calm absence of self-destructiveness is a useful model for us humans who so often (both individually and collectively) seem possessed by the attractions of mass suicide.

This quality of resonant metaphor attracted me to write about boxelder bugs. Emerson, too, would have enjoyed the clarity, sanity, and directness of their lives, had Concord been fortunate enough to have boxelder trees. They go about the business of staying alive without hysteria, greed, or violence, but rather with a modest and courteous self-possession: they don't want to cause you trouble; they don't want to get in your way; they don't ask much of your hospitality; they clearly do not intend to let you kill them. Humans are in need of such models.

Whitman said: "A mouse is miracle enough to stagger sextillions of infidels." So is a boxelder bug.

THE BOXELDER BUG PRAYS

I want so little
For so little time,
A south window,
A wall to climb,
The smell of coffee,
A radio knob,
Nothing to eat,
Nothing to rob,
Not love, not power,
Not even a penny.
Forgive me only
For being so many.

Boxelder bugs as one of the archstones of human community, illustrated by brief journeys to three strange places on our planet

I. SUNDAY IN IOWA

After the prayers,
in Swedish, of course,

> *I Jesu namn*
> *går vi till bord*
> *ätta, dricka*
> *på Gud's ord.*
> *Gud till ära*
> *oss till gagn*
> *så får vi mat*
> *I Jesu namn.*

Father passed the chicken
calmly to Uncle LeRoy and then
flattened with his thumb
the boxelder bug making his slow
way toward the mashed potatoes.
"Democrats," he said,
"Democrats . . . " in a voice
quite different from the prayers.

II. Monday in Minnesota

The menu in the Comfy Cafe Reads:

> Beef Dinner
> Beef Commercial
> Beef Hot Dish
> Beef Sandwich
> Beef Soup

Four bib overalls topped
by four seed corn hats,
consider the options, gravely,
silently, like judges
about to hang a murderer.
Finally, one stubs out
his smoke on the back of
the boxelder bug who crawled
into the ashtray.
"God-damn Republicans," he says,
"I'll have the Commercial."

III. Tuesday in the central African rain-forest

Among the pygmies,
cripples and dope smokers
who spoil the hunt
stay home; their job:
take blame if women
scorch the stew, elephant
gets away, love-making
goes poorly, wind
blows out the fire. The more
cursed and spat on,
the better they feel.
Only used gods sing:
"I am despised and rejected by men;
I am why things have gone
wrong for so long."

Some likely places to look for a Boxelder bug should your life ever conspire to give you the necessity, or desire, or both

I

He crawls over bristles on
the ear of the old man who snores
in the pew in front of you
while the sermon slowly vaporizes
into the invisible aether
of grace and disembodied love.
The bug is, on the other hand,
still clearly visible.

II

He bushwhacks across the gold sweater
on the girl reading alone at the desk.
At last discovers her breast and goes
around and around and around and around and
   around,
pulling your eye behind him like the weak
climber slowly belayed to the summit.

III

On the TV screen he
is the moving spot who is not
electric, slow enough
to be truly alive. Under
his belly, laughter erupts,
but he plods on, a moon
walker in a winged spacesuit
who turned off mission
control at last.

ONE USE A PRACTICAL CIVILIZATION MIGHT MAKE OF THEM

The stripes lifted off
the backs of boxelder bugs
in a single house in the middle
of the North American continent laid
end to end would make a narrow
red highway past the moon; . . .
on this road, the poor, the ugly,
the sick, the disagreeable, could drive
away into the universe. . . .

It is sometimes difficult to keep in mind that boxelder bugs are not the only amazing and unlikely creatures in the universe

I

"I don't know how anything so dry
as those bugs can be alive."

II

Yahweh, Mohammed, and Jesus
all bloomed in the desert.

III

And the saguaro cactus —
the worst lizards —

And they are useful too

They entertain the cat
who's too slow for flies.

Asked why, of all things, I write poems about boxelder bugs, I invoke the ghost of my mother, who had more than her share of Icelandic wisdom

Jona used nylon stockings as rope,
made cats out of beer bottles and light bulbs,
Christmas angels from rolled up newspapers,
patched the patches on patches on underwear
till they turned into clown suits,
polished shoes with old socks,
and rosemaled coffee cans.
You never know, she said,
when it might come in handy,
and you can always put it in soup
where it'll taste good.
In the thirties, she canned pigeons,
made gravy with chicken feet.
Old torn pants turned into quilts,
and pillows were stuffed with hair.
Don't waste what little you've got, she said.
Hard times are coming again; someday
you'll be hungry and poor,
sorry for what you throw away
or ignore.

Isak Dinesen, when she was old, dined only on oysters, white grapes, and champagne. The boxelder bug, too, practices a parsimonious though elegant diet

The bug slides
out from behind
the radio dial
where all winter
he lived
eating music.

To continue Emerson's essays
NATURE AND *THE POET*

Nature is thrifty; wastes nothing.
There is always the right number
of boxelder bugs, in the right
places. The poet's eye should be
likewise economical. Let him
cease complaining that the world
is without objects fit to become
his subject. He could live two
centuries and not exhaust a
boxelder bug, seen right. The
question is always and only how
quickly a single boxelder bug
would exhaust himself on the
whole tribe of poets.

A little boxelder counterpoint to clear the palate between courses of words, in which certain not entirely original themes are combined with the bug's motive in unexpected ways. To be played by three players on instruments of their choice, sung by three singers, played on one keyboard, or read in silence by a mental virtuoso.

In pursuit of the true bug, poetry queries biology; and discovers that every just metaphor is exact science. A talk with Charles Hamrum, Entomologist

Beyond this whimsy of metaphor lives science, the true bug. Fact is one more circular road toward the boxelder bug, or, as Emerson says:

> A subtle chain of countless rings
> The next unto the farthest brings;
> The eye reads omens where it goes,
> And speaks all languages the rose;
> And striving to be man, the worm
> Mounts through all the spires of form.

Boxelder bugs, like Icelanders and Arabian horses, have impressive geneology.

Class: Insecta
Subclass: Euenthomata
Superorder: Hemipteroidea
Order: Hemiptera (Half-winged, called *true* bugs; to distinguish them from false bugs?)
Suborder: Terrestrial Bugs (Geocorisae: land bugs with conspicuous antennae and an ejaculatory bulb in the male.)
Family: Coreidae (Leaf-footed bugs)
Species: Leptocoris trivitattus (Boxelder bugs)

His brothers and sisters in this family include: minute pirate bugs, swallow bugs, bed bugs, bat bugs, damsel bugs, assassin bugs, ambush bugs, water striders, ripple bugs, velvet water bugs, water measurer bugs, stilt bugs, lace bugs, shield bugs, harlequin bugs, and one-spot stink bugs. After humans desert this planet, enough relatives will be left in this single true bug family to divide labor, staff universities, and maintain New York at its current level of size and activity. No one who has observed boxelder bugs dancing their pavane in a south window lacks confidence that ballet will prosper as never before in this new civilization.

Hemiptera are an old order: they have existed at least since the triassic, one hundred eighty to two hundred thirty million years ago. As contemporaries of the snapping turtle, the hammerhead shark, and the horseshoe crab, they saw dinosaurs rise and fall as masters of the earth. Perhaps a cellular memory of brontosaurus prevents them from being sufficiently afraid of humans. They own information we long to wring from bones or read in fossils.

Humans have discovered 23,000 different species of true bugs; 4,500 live with us in America. How many species of us have they discovered? Does an epicanthic fold, kinked hair, or freckled pink skin make much difference to a boxelder bug? Can they tell which are the deadly members of our species? Are the sexual differences that so obsess us apparent to a hemipteran eye? Do they recognize breasts?

~~~

I went to a biologist and asked him questions for which there might indeed be answers. Charles Hamrum was my biology teacher twenty-five years ago at Gustavus Adolphus, a college in southern Minnesota. A wry and witty man, and an entomologist by training, he loves and praises curiosity where he finds it. I distinguished myself among his students only by an obtuse refusal to remember names of parts of living things. Experience improved my attitude in this regard, as I think he always suspected it might. I spoke to him on a rainy Sunday night in April after he returned from incubating eggs and tending flocks of odd geese. Punctuate this little interview with ferocious thunder cracks, hard rain slapping the window, and laughter.

Poet: What do boxelder bugs eat?
Biologist: The boxelder tree, like all maples, is very generous with its seeds. The bugs drill a hole through the seed coat with the stylets of their beaks; then they spit in it, dissolve the goodies, and aspirate it back up again.
Poet: A biologist up in Brainard told me you had to have a female tree to get bugs; no seeds in the male.
Biologist: I don't know, but if that's the case, we must have nothing but females around here.
Poet: What's their life cycle, their life expectancy like?
Biologist: They're a damned energy-conscious little bug. They lay their eggs in spring, spend summer in the tree. They use

the loose shaggy bark for shade against sun scald, and to hide from the woodpeckers who might get hungry. Most bugs would have another generation between growing and hibernating. That would increase their chances of survival: one generation to hedge your bets, and another one to deliver the goods. But not boxelder bugs. They're gamblers. They over-winter.

Poet: In my house?

Biologist: Sure. Freezing is for dumb bugs.

Poet: Why are they so dry? Don't they ever drink?

Biologist: Not much. They sneak a drink now and then, like most of us, but they're good water conservation bugs.

Poet: What does it mean to be a "true bug?"

Biologist: Classifications don't amount to much. Nobody really agrees on that stuff. Better to look at things one at a time. But generally, they're six-legged, half-winged, with sucking mouth parts, partial hibernators. Actually, there's a kind of ecological radiation going on in bug groups. Three families split up the functions: predators, plant suckers, and seed eaters. Boxelder bugs eat seeds.

Poet: I'm curious whether they think. I told a state legislator from western Minnesota I was writing a book about boxelder bugs, and he expressed the hope that I wasn't doing it with state funds. Then he said, "Even if they're a pest, they're a damn smart little bug." "What do you mean?", I asked. "Most bugs," he said, "will run into a brick fifty times in a row, and never figure out that it's there, but every time a boxelder bug walks across the table when I'm eating, I put a fork down before I squash him. By God, the bug walks up to the fork and stops. He wobbles his antennae a little and walks right around the fork just as if he knew what it was. Now most bugs will walk right up the fork tines and fall through just as if it was a cattle guard. But the boxelder bug is too smart to waste time on that stuff." That's his story. Can they think?

Biologist: Henri Fabre wondered about that, too. Do you know that great essay about the pine processionaires where he gets pine beetles marching in a circle with their nose in each other's hind end for nine days, waiting for one to break the chain and start out on his own?

Poet: I love Fabre. [Fabre was a French natural historian of the nineteenth century, the author of an enormous ten-volume work, *Souvenirs of the Insects*. He was a poor man, an elementary teacher with minimal training, who wanted to know whether insects thought. At fifty-six years old, he came into a few acres in southern France, and there watched bugs with great patience and intelligence, sometimes for days, afterwards writing lovely prose without the baggage of scientific jargon to describe what he saw. He was an old man without even a microscope, only a passion to know insects, and a sense of humor. He finished his book at eighty-eight.]

Biologist: Scientists never trusted Fabre, you know, though he was right about almost everything. He treated us as if we were part of nature too, but in his time, people wanted to think of themselves as God's exclusive children, no connection to insects.

Poet: So can they think?

Biologist: They have memory, not thought.

Poet: Do bugs see?

Biologist: In 1910, a German named Exener dissected out the crystalline portion of the eyelet facet of a dragonfly's eye, and adapted it to the lens of a box camera; with that he took a sharp picture of the spire of Cologne cathedral. That pretty well disproved the idea that bugs are blind.

Poet: Can they hear?

Biologist: Like us, they have a tympanum, a chordotonal organ that vibrates. It screens out all kinds of racket except what they really have to hear: the mating call. A beautiful rendition of Bach wouldn't mean squat to them.

Poet: I've argued otherwise, particularly with the bugs who live in my piano. They know when I play well.

Biologist: Things must be different in Minneota.

Poet: What about smell?

Biologist: That's their best sense. A lot of the boxelder bug's rela-

tives smell bad, but not them. They're not true stink bugs.

Poet: And they're not dirty?

Biologist: Oh, they shit on the curtains a little.

Poet: Any size limits?

Biologist: Vernon Wigglesworth wrote a book, *Insect Physiology*, where he described doing surgery on the glands of a bug's thorax. It stopped them from going into their adult stage. They just went on eating and molting, eating and molting, eating and molting, until he finally had to take them out on a leash to walk them around the neighborhood.

Poet: What!

Biologist: Well, that was my line. But the bugs did keep growing to outrageous size. They finally got so big that it broke down their legs to carry that body mass.

Poet: The same would happen to a forty foot human, I suppose. What does a boxelder bug look like under a microscope?

Biologist: Looks sort of like a big boxelder bug. Actually, to see them under a microscope, you have to dissect them, pull the legs out with a tweezer, pull the eyes out. When you're down to the thorax, you check out one side, and then turn it over to play the flip side.

Poet: Sort of a small disc of celestial music. Is there any evolutionary reason for the decorative red stripe on the wing?

Biologist: Probably . . . [Thunder] I'm totally seduced by natural selection. If it does not help them now, it did in the past.

  *   *   *   *   *

Not the poet but the biologist speaks poetry. Whoever owns fact owns the bricks to build imagination. To see and feel boxelder bugs, imagine three roads, the three ideas that run through this book: the poetry of experience (observation, memory); the poetry of fact (learning, science); the poetry of the invisible (music, the soul).

All three roads arrive at the same place, and you can travel them in any sequence. If you start on any of them and are persistent, you will arrive at the end of all of them.

Poets and Scientists Find Boxelder Bugs Useful for Both Metaphor and Experiment

Crush a boxelder bug.
After the little snap
a tiny liquid drop
the color of honey comes
out on your thumb.
The boxelder bug does not
hear this sound.
The red racing stripes on
his black back, like decorated
running shoes, finally don't
run anywhere, anymore.
You, on the other hand, have done
what your life prepared you for:
kill something useless and innocent,
and try to find some beauty in it.

THE MINNEOTA UNDERTAKER, THINKING PERHAPS OF FUTURE BUSINESS, LOOKS ME SQUARE IN THE EYE DURING MEN'S NIGHT AT THE GOLF COURSE, AND SAYS:

I thought of you last night
as I flicked a boxelder bug
off my lapel.

HE REMINDS ME, SOMETIMES, OF THE ANGEL OF DEATH, MY OWN DYBBUK

The boxelder bug lands
on my left hand
and explores,
moves around slowly
among pink hairs,
a tumor with red veins
who wants a campsite
but can't make up his mind
quite where to kill me.
All this he does
with no malice.
It's his work.

THOUGH DIFFICULT, IT IS POSSIBLE TO KILL BOXELDER BUGS. IF YOU ARE INTERESTED, YOU MIGHT TRY THIS METHOD

Take two bricks.
Creep deliberately up
Behind the boxelder bug,
Being careful not to sing—
This will alert him.
In a graceful flowing gesture,
Something like a golf swing
Or reaching for your lover in the dark,
Gather up the boxelder bug
On the surface of the left brick
Bringing the right brick
At the same time firmly down
Together with the left brick.
There will be a loud crashing,
Like broken cymbals,
Maybe a breaking of brick, and
If you are not careful,
Your own voice rising.
When the brick dust has settled
And you have examined your own hands,
Carefully,
You will not see the boxelder bug,
There is a small hole in the brick
And he is exploring it,
Calmly, like a millionaire
In an antique shop.

SINCE EVERY WEAPON FROM THE STONE TO
THE CLUB TO THE WOODEN HORSE TO THE
AX TO THE MUSKET TO THE AIRPLANE TO
THE PESTICIDE HAS FINALLY GOTTEN USED
FOR WHAT IT WAS REALLY INTENDED, AFTER
THE RETIRED ACTORS OF HISTORY FROM
CAESAR TO ATTILA TO OLAF TO GENGHIS
TO IVAN TO NAPOLEON TO MUSSOLINI TO
JOHNSON TO THIS VERY DAY HAVE LIED TO
THE SUCKERS ABOUT THE PEACETIME USES OF
AXES FOR CUTTING WOOD AND GUNPOWDER
FOR DRAGON PARADES AND THE BALANCE OF
POWER AND THE DEFENSE OF LIBERTY, AND
THE SUCKERS HAVE BOUGHT IT AND
MARCHED OFF TEN YEARS LATER WITH THE
SAME WEAPONS IN THEIR HANDS TO KILL
OFF THE SAME VARIETY OF SUCKER WHO
BELIEVED THE SAME PHONY STORY IN THE
NEXT TOWNSHIP ON THE PLANET, WHAT
INSUFFERABLE ARROGANCE MAKES US NOBLE
AMERICANS IMAGINE THAT WE CAN
CONTRADICT THE CLEAR EVIDENCE OF TEN
THOUSAND YEARS OF THE HISTORY OF
HUMAN BEHAVIOR AND NOT BLOW EACH
OTHER THE HELL OFF THIS PLANET
LEAVING ONLY:

Cockroaches in the blowing grass
finding new things to eat,
naming each blade their own way now.
Maybe also boxelder bugs.
Everyone forgets them —
Could this forget them too?
Maybe their power to ignore
our food, our music, our cant,
was really the long preparing
to live without touching anything
men ever blackened with the lie
about whether they really wanted
to do it to each other at last.

Boxelder Bug Variations   29

A LADY FROM MONTEVIDEO DESCRIBES HER STRUGGLE WITH BOXELDER BUGS

It started with cold war;
Now we've moved to detente —

The poet recommends surrender.
Then joy.

CHARLIE SMITH, THE MANDOLIN PLAYER, REVEALS AN UNEXPECTED STREAK OF CRUELTY TOWARD BOXELDER BUGS, BUT TAKES TWO OF THE THREE STEPS NECESSARY FOR ATTAIN- ING FULL MORAL CONSCIOUSNESS

I

At school we glued up
their wings and set them on fire.
God, we were awful!

II

No, merely human. . . .
Awful is much too easy
a consolation.

BOXELDERS ON PARADE

brisk march time

THE BOXELDER BUG TAKES HIS STAND ON THE PRO-LIFE ISSUE AND ITS ROOTS IN INDUSTRIAL CAPITALISM

Among boxelder bugs,
democracy does not consist
in flattening neighbors
between Bible pages,
or circling the gold bag,
drawstrings clamped
between antennae.
They use no text
to club the peculiar,
nor do they speculate
in anything but sun;
whatever market they buy in
is always glutted.
In only one regard are we
each other's mirror:
They admire their own
wings too much, believe
in never-ending trees.
Dry feathery corpses
fill window after window
until the sun goes black.
The boxelder prophet sings:
Leave earth alone; give
rooms and mountains air
to breathe, one wing
lifted toward sun is
praise of God. A million
together is a shroud.

I COME BACK TO MY HOUSE, AND FIND THIS EMBLEM OF MORTALITY WAITING FOR ME WITH A NOTE: "I DIDN'T DO IT. JOHN ALLEN."

The boxelder bug crawls
into apricot shampoo
and drowns.
In this thick orange ocean
he will tread water
forever and never
reach bottom,
red stripes turning
over and over,
skinny legs splayed out in
this hopeless butterfly
stroke toward nowhere.

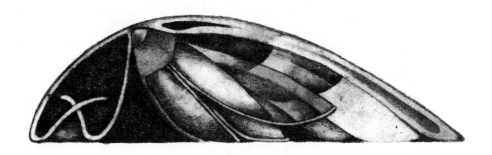

Some explanations (not found in Darwin) for the origin of the species

I

Dandruff fallen off
the sleeping troll's hair;
his shoulder is buried,
under your house.

II

Pacifist neutrons
deserted the bomb
before it exploded,
had no wish
to bear wings
against their neighbor.

Nuclear physicists use astounding comparisons to make clear the nature of infinite numbers

An adult male Norwegian
weighs as much as
two and a half billion
boxelder bugs.
Is it any surprise that
there are more boxelder bugs
than Norwegians?
Imagine a planet in which
Norwegians crawled up
and down your kitchen walls
by the thousands, hid
under the warm coffee pot,
fell like discolored noodles out
of the noodle bags where they slept;
after the blizzards started,
you would find Norwegians
dried inside light fixtures, Norwegians
clogging up the vacuum cleaner,
Norwegians floating in
cups of lukewarm coffee.

THOUGH HOUSEWIVES AND SCRUPULOUS PEOPLE OFTEN THINK OF THEM AS PESTS, THERE ARE CERTAIN ADVANTAGES IN HAVING BOXELDER BUGS AROUND

In a house with boxelder bugs
you're never lonely;
quiet neighbors who
leave whiskey alone,
don't wake you at night
with drunk stories of old
girlfriends, lives
gone wrong, new poems.
Boxelder bugs don't pay
much attention to whether
you get your work done.

As it says in pamphlets
from various churches
and helping professions,
they are just there
whenever they are needed,
whether they are wanted,
just there
                    And there   And there
                              And there

                    And there

          And there   And there

     And there

                                        And there
And there   And there

                         And there

In the Church of Boxelder Bugs, Sermons are not Exactly as One has Been Led to Expect by Experience Among the Lutherans

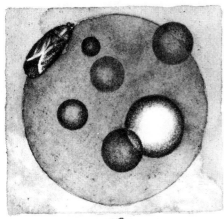

In 1731, the Fourth Earl of Orrery built a contraption of metal balls and wood to show the relative speed and position of the planets then known to revolve around the sun in this solar system. They were six: Mercury, Venus, Earth, Mars, Jupiter, and Saturn. It was known that they were of different sizes, that they moved in different orbits, that they did not collide with one another, but moved harmoniously. The Orrery was, and is, in fact, a mobile statue of the planetary dance.

In 1750, Johann Sebastian Bach died blind, leaving incomplete by a few bars his greatest work, *Art of Fugue*, a series of elaborate fugues based on a bare — indeed boring — theme:

It is in common time, consists of a simple triad and four notes of a scale going up and then coming down. It goes nowhere, except back around on itself, like an awkward man who doesn't know what to say when told that he is loved. Bach deals with this theme in an altogether astonishing way. He exhausts it in order to see what can be made of *it*, of the idea of fugue, and of music itself. He composed, in fact, a kind of encyclopedia which is, at the same time, a dance.

In the seventh counterpoint, he makes the theme move against itself simultaneously in six different ways: in its original form and time, at twice its own speed, at half its own speed, and combined in various ways with the original theme upside down in normal time, and again at both half and twice its own speed. Listeners, unless they study the piece, do not notice this. They hear instead a calm and harmonious dance in which everything is measured and simple. What they hear, in fact, is the exact musical equivalent of looking at an Orrery: six planets dancing together with great calm. This piece of music is amazing as the solar system itself.

Those six planets danced together inside Bach's head. This is not a sentimental opinion but a simple fact, as any physicist will confirm. Emerson, nearly one hundred years after the invention of the Orrery, wrote in *Nature* that words are signs of natural facts, and natural facts the signs of spiritual facts. Again, modern physics confirms this intuition, thus demonstrating that a man who knows that a farm is nothing but a mute gospel knows something about astronomy and counterpoint as well as agriculture and religion.

Western Minnesota farms are full of boxelder trees, and the south farmhouse windows full of boxelder bugs. Indeed, they are a kind of live Orrery, a mute *Art of Fugue*, a gospel. At any given time while I write in this kitchen, six boxelder bugs move on their six spindly legs in six different though harmonious rhythms. This takes place in my line of sight — or as Emerson would say: in my angle of vision. They do not hurry, but do not quite stop either. They dance with some invisible partner. Think of a waltz in turn-of-the-century Vienna: a marble ballroom, late at night, glimmering candle shadows. A string sextet saws the air with bows — but they play a *Blue Danube* made entirely of silence. Six dancers in evening dress move around the parquet floor, but though their arms are held out in the proper way, there are no partners. Nothing, at any rate, we hear with the ear, or see with the eye.

But solve the mystery of the ballroom in this way: name the dancers: swaggering Mars, fat sleepy Jupiter, wiry darting Mercury, vain Saturn looking around for followers, melancholy Earth seeming ready to immolate himself, Venus swaying her antennae sensually. Now you hear it: the strings saw away at Counterpoint VII.

Bach loved mathematics — secret signs made of numbers, and the astonishing coincidences that arise from them — both in music, and in the world, if, indeed, the two are different. We would probably now call his mathematics numerology, though that does not seem dignified enough to me. It is, at any rate, at least as exact a way of describing the world as astrology, phrenology, psychology, physics, or religion.

This is not an exhaustive list. Bach wrote six of each:
1) Brandenburg Concertos
2) French Suites
3) English Suites
4) Keyboard Partitas
5) Solo Violin Partitas
6) Solo Cello Suites
7) Flute Sonatas
8) Violin Sonatas
9) Trio Sonatas for Keyboard
10) Christmas Cantatas in the Oratorio

His most complex and learned fugue, the ricercar that ends *The Musical Offering*, has six independent voices singing the same tune at different pitches and speeds. To make six independent voices playable by a single keyboard player, and clearly audible to any listener, was considered virtually impossible until Bach accomplished it.

Here are some more facts:
1) The boxelder bug has six legs.
2) There are six musical pitches in the name Boxelder Bug: B,E,D,E,B,G
3) There are six pitches in the theme of the *Art of Fugue*.
4) For most of human history, six visible planets moved around our small star.

Make of these facts whatever you will; neither your government's defense strategies, your university education, nor your minister's sermons, will decide the truth, falsehood, or the connection between these facts. These numerical coincidences are as likely to be alive with truth as an official press release or Papal Bull.

Where, then, is the sun around which Bach's planets move, or which gives a center to this dance of six feet of six moving boxelder bugs? The sun is almost continuously invisible. Half its life, wherever you are, is night; as in Zeno's paradox, half the remaining sun is shrouded in clouds; for half of the half still left, it is so brilliant you dare not look at it, but must feel it on the skin of your back. So for half of the half of the half left, you see it rise sometimes and sink at others if you're attentive enough either to get up early or look late. Yet not even the President has denied the existence of sun, or light, or heat.

Bach would probably have called the sun around which his six visible voices dance: God. I would not call it by this name. The boxelder bugs have not told me, or you either, what they call it, but I have the feeling, and have had for years, that they know the right name, and if we could hear them, it would begin the next human leaping upwards.

contrapunctus II

A little boxelder counterpoint to clear the palate between courses of words, in which certain not entirely original themes are combined with the bug's motive in unexpected ways. To be played by three players on instruments of their choice, sung by three singers, played on one keyboard, or read in silence by a mental virtuoso.

THE AFTERLIFE, OR THE GREAT MANDALA (TAKE YOUR CHOICE) ILLUSTRATED BY A BOXELDER BUG WHO GETS IT INTO HIS WINGS TO TRAVEL

A boxelder bug slides into the Yellow Medicine River in Minneota, rides the current like a water skier down to Granite Falls, tumbles into the Minnesota, follows the old Sioux trail to Minneapolis. Brown water begins smelling odd, and 2-4-D and sewage almost finish him off, but he crawls inside a rusty Grain Belt can, floats past Shakopee to Fort Snelling, finally gets into the Mississippi, peers out from his beer can, decides to wing his way onto the back of a wheat barge bound for New Orleans, eyes bluffs through twenty-seven locks and dams, south of St. Louis drifts into Huck's and Jim's slave country. At New Orleans the barge unloads onto a giant freighter bound for Bergen. Cocking antennae in thanks for the ride, he dives into the salt Gulf Stream, suns his wings through the Caribbean, sleeps a while, wakes up east of Newfoundland, enjoying weather less, but kept alive by his warm ocean river. Cold when he sails into Bergen, he crawls around the harbor a day or two, thinking it looks like Minneota with salt water and too many mountains. He plunges into the Gulf Stream's feeble tail for the run north to Spitsbergen. At this point, he stops. In a world turned white, his stripe seems the only red for a thousand miles. He sees something else black, crawls for it with the last energy in his almost frozen legs. He mounts the black spot. It breathes . . . the nose of an ice bear taking a nap. The bear yawns, and the boxelder bug disappears into his stomach. After a while, the bear kills a seal with a single swipe of its paw, gorges itself, shits,

and sleeps again. A Canada goose, migrating south, spots warm bear
scat, swoops down to the ice, waddles over to investigate, sees
something moving and snatches it up in his bill. Continuing south,
the goose winds up at Lac Qui Parle, where a hunter who decided to
brave the game warden shoots him. Soon the goose is gutted and
plucked in Minneota, and the hunter's wife, in her worried haste,
hardly notices the familiar bug crawl sleepily out, make his way
down to the park where the Yellow Medicine slogs along to Granite
Falls. . . . and . . .

Minnesota Winters Are Difficult for Creatures Whose Weight Cannot Be Measured in Stones

A boxelder bug surprised out
in west wind at forty below
rode swirling snow
clean out of Minnesota,
wound up embalmed in
an ice cube in Pennsylvania,
scared hell out of the lady
who found red stripes in her gin
and tonic, thought she'd seen
the face of God.

A REASON TO PREFER THE COMPANY OF BOXELDER BUGS, AND GREET THEIR RETURN WITH PRAISE

After the killing frost,
boxelder bugs return,
regular as religion,
into curtains, coffee, sunlight,
minding their business
without comment.

Maybe they are in charge
of counting leaves blowing
past the south window.
I won't ask; they
won't tell; the old fellowship
blossoms between us.

Kafka only imagined it

Sometimes I roll over in bed,
think I've turned into one.
They outnumber me by so many,
live more peacefully in my house
than I do myself.
No ghosts for them;
chairs rocking in the dark.
At night, they crawl into me —
carry food and ideas
from brain to thigh
to spleen to finger.
Early in the morning
my hands go by themselves
to the piano, begin
playing music I've never heard before.

Boxelder Bug Variations

THE VARIETIES OF INSECT SPEECH

I

The Madagascar cockroach,
three inches long, emits
hisses heard up to twelve feet
away, pumping up his belly,
expelling out air through
modified flank vents.

II

The boxelder bug on
the other hand
says nothing.

SOME COUNTRIES, BY VIRTUE OF HARSH GEOGRAPHY AND THE ABSENCE OF TREES, ARE DEPRIVED OF THEIR COMPANY

In Iceland
No boxelder bugs

Hungry birds
Lonesome houses

No frogs
Either

Silent water
All night

48

THE BOXELDER BUG: HIS CLAVICHORD

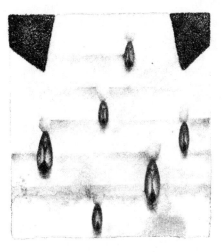

If a boxelder bug had ever taken up the keyboard as a profession, he would have played the clavichord. It is the oldest, simplest, and quietest keyboard, closer to silence than a grand piano. You make sound not by striking or plucking the string with hammer or plectrum, but by pressing against it with a dull brass tangent. The string vibrates quietly for its entire length until it is gently muffled in soft felt and dies. The felt simply waits by the pin block for the sound to come shivering into it; it does nothing. Piano dampers move on a heavy steel bar, full of bolts and pins, rising and falling to head off vibrations before they crash into each other. Harpsichord sound dies down with a dull thud when the weight of the jack pulls the hard leather damper abruptly next to the string. These mechanisms have virtues, one not superior to the other. Heavy dampers give the piano weight, brilliance, and variety; gravity's thud gives the harpsichord bite and clarity; simple felt wound between strings gives the clavichord almost-silence and soulfulness.

The clavichord trembles, and in this resembles the human voice more than other keyboards. Its sound is like grass moving around in the wind, or a curtain billowing into your bedroom at dawn, or the little body shiver when lovemaking is over. The old Germans loved this effect and called it *Bebung*. To do it, press the key, hold it, moving your finger gently up and down without allowing the note to stop sounding. This requires a certain delicate small muscle coordination. A boxelder bug would be very good at it. Those intense keyboard ariosos by Bach begin to make sense when you play them with this effect. They sound like a wonderful contralto, full of feeling and intelligence, singing "Schlafe Mir," or "Erbarme Dich."

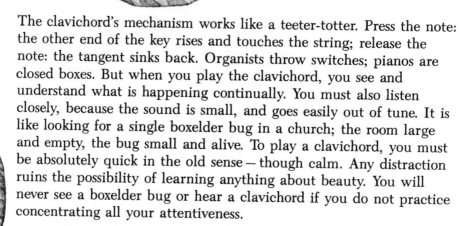

The clavichord's mechanism works like a teeter-totter. Press the note: the other end of the key rises and touches the string; release the note: the tangent sinks back. Organists throw switches; pianos are closed boxes. But when you play the clavichord, you see and understand what is happening continually. You must also listen closely, because the sound is small, and goes easily out of tune. It is like looking for a single boxelder bug in a church; the room large and empty, the bug small and alive. To play a clavichord, you must be absolutely quick in the old sense — though calm. Any distraction ruins the possibility of learning anything about beauty. You will never see a boxelder bug or hear a clavichord if you do not practice concentrating all your attentiveness.

The clavichord, once you begin playing it, is always slightly out of tune; at rest though, it possesses a kind of theoretical, abstract intonation. But the smallest weight — a boxelder bug or a child's finger — pushes a chord out of its just tuning. A piano is a heavy machine tuned by an electronic gadget so that the middle A vibrates 440 times per second until weather intervenes. To play an A at 440 on a clavichord, you must press the key at precisely that weight; if too violent, you vibrate 445 times, sharping the note; if too timid, the note sinks flat, to 435. In *Bebung*, the A wavers back and forth wildly around the pitch. That trembling is always a little cacaphonous; to play 440, you must count 440, and neither you nor the boxelder bug can do that. But mechanical precision has little to do with the beauty of the noises you make! The note is always imperfect, but what you do in playing, unconsciously after a while, is make that imperfection harmonious with what happens around it in the chord or line. This is what you do in living your own life decently. Feeling is everything in playing the clavichord; as the old Germans remind us — soul and passion in a music close to silence, not steely synthesizer precision!

Clavichords cannot be recorded very accurately. To really hear one, you must play it yourself, or sit close to the player on the same bench. At normal sound recording levels, noises from the player's fingers and the mechanism itself are louder than the music; if the recording engineer is careful, what you hear sounds like a keyed harp or guitar, lovely, but not much like the clavichord. This is an

experience you can't have vicariously. I think Bach might have been glad that his favorite instrument so successfully resists industrial technology. Like the boxelder bug, it finished evolving, reached a kind of artistic and biological simplicity that the universe decided not to risk improving. It is a still point in a turning world.

The clavichord died in the eighteenth century because it could not drown out the noise around it — hammers, steam engines, revolutions, factories, trumpets, cities. It is an instrument for a silent corner of an empty house with only boxelder bugs as neighbors; or to play in the woods at night, no one for miles around; an instrument either for the rich who buy silence and privacy in old villas; or for the poor who own little, live invisible lives, and make do with the simple. It is not an instrument for the middle class, who long to display bright goods, and hear the sociable racket of cities. You listen best in some created wilderness, a garden maybe — not a concert hall. For concerts of clavichord music, wear, like the boxelder bug, only the red stripes on your own back.

Skeptics who hear the near silence of the clavichord described are always astonished when they hear its real quietness; a stomach growling, water running out of a faucet, whispered conversation, all drown it out. Yet the silvery penetration in the sound, if you listen with full attention for half an hour, begins to seem louder than the Wanamaker organ or the Boston Symphony. A vigorous chord is sufficient to bring you off your seat or terrify you. What happens, I think, is something like looking for a long time at a single boxelder bug. You take the music inside yourself: while the outer ear shrinks, the inner one grows enormously. This interior sound, born of complete attention, makes your senses alive in some old way you thought you'd forgotten. A glass of water becomes old whiskey, a woman's hand on your shoulder is as much eros as you can stand without bursting, sunlight falling on your book is a gold temple wall. After a half hour of this, a piano sounds vulgar and cheap; thirty seconds of a rock band would make you an anchorite for life. You can't play the clavichord all the time; it would unsuit you for the twentieth century. Blake's sunflower blazed for only a few seconds. Boxelder bugs disappear into light and silence.

I love the clavichord best of all keyboard instruments, for that silence, privacy, and imperfection. Music written for it from the sixteenth through the eighteenth century tends to be romantic and inward. Fast dance tunes and bravura flourishes don't go well on it.

It is an instrument to play with grass, mountains, and water listening. Boxelder bugs are good company for clavichord music. They move slowly, make no noise, are small and modest — but they are alive, and if our ears were acute enough, we could hear their hearts beating, breath coming in and out, sucking in the same air we do, all night, asleep. To be alive and to know it is everything. Everything.

II

Whenever words scratched on a page get too heavy and intractable, or newspapers full of old mistakes seem made of lead or sandpaper in my hands, I begin to experience the longing to invent something invisible, so I compose music. Following the trail of boxelder bugs was not as easy as I imagined, since they frequently disappeared into light too brilliant for me to follow. At that point, I threw the scratched pages of poetry on the music stand of my clavichord, and began playing Bach or improvising in order to plow snow off mental highways and make a track back into the imagination. Probably not the first, or second, but the fiftieth time that I looked up at my own handwriting, I saw six musical notes in the bug's name, and played them, first in a normal sequence, then upside down, backwards, both upside down and backwards, as the theme of a waltz, ragtime, blues, gavotte, canon, gigue, polka; harmonizing them conventionally, oddly, unspeakably; combining them in counterpoint with hymns, folk tunes, snatches of classical music I loved; moving them around on the keyboard from soprano, to alto, tenor, bass; slowing them down, speeding them up; making from them a pentatonic E minor chord; discovering that in sequence they fell nicely into the old Phrygian mode, the original mode of the great passion hymn "O Sacred Head Now Wounded/With Grief and Shame Laid Down."

Boxelder Bug Variations

Schumann used the same musical trick: taking random musical letters in a name, to make a kind of motto theme from them. In *Carnaval*, the same letters appear anagrammatically in his girlfriend's hometown, and in his own name: A, E^b, C, B, or in German, A, E^s, C, H. From this meager material, he makes a half hour of splendid music. This is at least as sensible as John Cage's idea of composing from the Chinese *Book of Changes*.

The great musical anagram is, of course, Bach's name, in German: B^b, A, C, B.

In one of the most serendipitous (though true) stories from music history, Bach introduced his own name as a counter subject in the last fugue he wrote down on paper before blindness came on him: the final counterpoint of *Art of Fugue*. He died before finishing it; it ends in midstroke, on the way to something we will never hear. Yet humans have tried to imagine how those last pages of Bach might have sounded, and Busoni, in *Fantasia Contrapunctistica*, was audacious enough to try to finish it. His solution is interesting, and proves him a brave and intelligent man, though not Bach. Next to the size of Bach, we are, I suppose, all boxelder bugs of one variety or another.

Modern scholars now think that though the *Art of Fugue* is clearly abstract music to be read and contemplated as much as sounded, Bach designed it deliberately to be playable on a clavichord within the compass of a single player's hands. It is, at any rate, playable by one human willing to work at it, and thus becomes the greatest honor ever done the clavichord.

After a year of sporadic composing, I accumulated a set of clavichord variations on the boxelder bug motto longer than Beethoven's enormous *Diabelli*, or Bach's *Goldberg Variations*. This proved, if nothing else, that while I lacked their genius, I shared their persistence to economically exhaust my material, wringing every last possible shred of music from that sequence of six unpretentious notes.

I discovered, of course, that you can exhaust nothing in the universe. No matter how lazy or bored you become, no matter how tedious you think your corner of reality, and the random objects, both live and made, that nature conspired to put into your angle of vision, they have surprises for you. You have a soul, whether you want one or not, and when you open it to let it speak or hear, it becomes inexhaustible conversing with inexhaustible. The real meaning of free will is that we must choose, frequently with regret, to stop having one pleasure, and go on to another. Life, considered this way, is short, and we had better move around in it a bit before the next performance starts.

So, like all variation composers, I arrived at the "Big Fugue" in which everything you have said for however long you went on is combined, condensed, intensified, toward a conclusion which leaves an audience or innocent player flapping wings in delight. At about the same point in sketching the fugue that Bach reached in *Art of Fugue*, I discovered the true counterpoint that had lain under the boxelder bugs for all those centuries. It was Bach's name! My six notes and his four fit together like wood joints made by a brilliant carpenter. And I had not seen it till now — the simplest, therefore most elegant, harmonious, and true solution to the bug enigma. I had strained and wrenched the notes into every combination I could imagine, but only when I relaxed, in a way gave up and confessed good-humored defeat, did the true solution appear. I had finally learned a little of what boxelder bugs threatened to teach me from the first time I started looking at and thinking about them. They now imagined me!

After the Fugue, with the violent intellectual energy always necessary to make such a form work, I felt the need of a sigh before beginning the next leap into the unknown, so I composed a little lament on my leave-taking from Bach and the boxelder bug. Its sadness is really full of praise for the world, for you. Its justification is this: whatever you may think, there are never too many boxelder bugs in your house, nor too much clavichord music in the world. The universe planned things better than you think.

BACH'S ELDER LAMENT

As a boxelder bug bores inside a maple seed, so do variations burrow into the true music buried at the heart of even so trivial a theme as Anton Diabelli's waltz

Friends, hearing some of these poems, remarked that the connection between boxelder bugs and Beethoven's *Diabelli Variations* is not immediately apparent. This might be true, but only if one had not spent considerable time swatting boxelder bugs off a score while practicing. Pianists understand that both hands are required continually and vigorously to play the *Diabelli Variations*.

I am interested in the *idea* of Variation. It is a curious fact that often the most ingenious and intense pieces by the greatest composers, which seem to accumulate a lifetime's whole knowledge and feeling into themselves, are long sets of variations that begin with trifles, with nothing, and build enormous, sublime, ecstatic, often humorous structures. This is something like building Notre Dame with tinker toys. The architect stands back and smiles, inviting you to admire his fantastic powers. Bach begins with a little dance tune from a child's instruction book and, using the bass line, builds the *Goldberg Variations*, an hour of canons, fugues, dances, laments, bravura displays, and finally, a joke: he combines tune and bass with two vulgar folk tunes: "I Been So Long Without You, Honey," and "Cabbages and Rutabagas Have Driven Me Away." Schumann thinks of a couple of his girl friends' names and home towns, picks out the musical notes that happen to be in them, and makes *Carnaval*. But Beethoven's *Diabelli Variations* are in some ways the grandest and most wonderful of them all.

Diabelli was a commercial promoter in nineteenth-century music publishing, and a kind of composer to boot. He sent out his innocuous little waltz, and invited most of the well-known composers in Europe to contribute variations — proceeds to go to a charity. This is an idea that generally produces second-rate everybody! Beethoven, at his imaginative height in 1820, looked at the little ta-tum waltz with irony and disdain, reading it with deaf ears, but with one of the most powerful musical minds yet born on this planet. On second look, almost to dare himself, he thought: how would this trifle sound if I ground it up in my imagination?

The result, an hour and a half long, is not easy to describe. You study it, read it, play it, listen to it for many years, and it does not stop opening itself to you. This is the bottomless delight of the human intelligence working as well as it probably ever has worked. But it is funny — full of parody, satire, and wit of the broadest and roughest kind! All this sublime humor grows from a simple boxelder bug of a waltz heard from Beethoven's angle.

This is not the *Diabelli Variations*. It is praise of the intelligence and spiritual life that roll around under Beethoven, and, equally, under the boxelder bug; an experiment to see whether something as simple and unpretentious as this bug has the sublime and eternal underneath its wings, holding it up in its long march through this world.

PLAYING THE *DIABELLI VARIATIONS,*
I DISCOVER THAT THE SUBLIME
IS SOMETIMES APPARENT IN
THE UNPRETENTIOUS, IF YOU
LISTEN WITH THE
RIGHT EARS

I

On a piano full of boxelder bugs, I practice the *Diabelli Variations.*
Bugs crawl over it, trapped between keys, impaled on hammers,
plunging to death under the pedal. Some crawl onto the score, try
to make Beethoven into Ives by filling in chords, adding a
dissonance or two. I am not fooled. I flick them off lightly, go at C
Major like a man possessed.

II

The boxelder bugs waltz, flap their black wings, get their antennae
rhythm right, dream of going on the road, giving lessons, getting
rich. They understand the C-Major mind, know there are lots of
them out there, the boxelder-bug majority, waltzing together forever,
reaching for wallets, wings ruffling in unison.

III

This boxelder waltz crawled through cathedral jaws into the whale's
stomach, found juices so acid they melted it down into gold. That
stomach honors whatever is drowned and transformed inside it. The
poor waltz knew it would die, so it ate well before expiring into
music.

IV

Beethoven, I love being born on this planet with you: bending over
music paper, breath ripe with onions and cabbages, socks moldy on
your feet, gray ratty hair falling over your folded forehead, stone
ears stuffed with bugs, ear trumpet pointed inside, the barrel
exploding with laughter, that peculiar, joyful music of human
suffering.

contrapunctus III

A little boxelder counterpoint to clear the palate between courses of words, in which certain not entirely original themes are combined with the bug's motive in unexpected ways. To be played by three players on instruments of their choice, sung by three singers, played on one keyboard, or read in silence by a mental virtuoso.

Boxelder Bug Variations

Why there are so many (boxelder bugs and poems, etc.)

One thing
leads
to another . . .

Eleven boxelder bug Haiku

I

Careful if you kill him!
There may be an afterlife
for both of you.

Those black spots in your lamp?
Only bugs who didn't make it
into the next world.

Here's a bug trapped,
dried in a spider web.
Where's the spider?

That bug tickling grandpa's photo
can't tell the difference
between quick and dead. Can you?

Praying to Jesus, I note
the boxelder bug crawl
out of his shadow.

II

"Always tell fall's come —
That shed out back's so full of 'em
she moves around by herself."

"Ma put out coffee cans
full of water. Those bugs thought
they'd found the swimming hole."

III

Don't fret, bug,
I keep house . . .
casually.

Somehow these
boxelder bugs don't seem
Icelandic. . . .

　　　　　— Issa (Robert Hass)

IV

The piano string stops trembling
but boxelder bugs
keep dancing.

The boxelder bug —
another thing that will never
be my friend.

　　　　　— Basho (Robert Bly)

An incident hitherto overlooked by scholars of the life of Samuel Johnson who made the first great dictionary of our lovely English words

Boswell and Dr. Johnson walked, late one fall morning, through a park, Johnson, as usual, generalizing mightily as he ambled under the misty trees. Passersby noted his rolling gait, the great bobbing scarred head, the fierce *basso profundo* voice. The two discussed, or rather, Johnson orated on the possibility of human happiness in a fallen world, and how one might attain it. During one of Johnson's sallies, Boswell reached over and brushed off a handful of small bugs fallen from the trees above into Dr. Johnson's wig. More vigorous than he thought, he loosened the wig which now sat askew on the great doctor's head. One bug landed on Dr. Johnson's nose before resuming his journey downward.

"Pray, sir, what are you doing to my wig?" queried Johnson.

"Only ridding you, sir, of a number of troublesome insects that have fallen on us from these trees."

"Insects, sir? Insects?"

"Yes, sir. An insect which inhabits one of your English trees. They are not precisely noxious, for their habits are only to crawl, to be present, and then to expire. They seem, sir, not like your English cockroach, inclined to share our dinner, but only to inhabit us. They are boxelder bugs."

While Boswell spoke, Dr. Johnson reached to straighten his wig, and while doing so, rescued the small bug from his nose. He raised the bug up to within a half-inch of his bulging, watery, half-blind eyes, and began examining it almost with tenderness. The bug moved calmly through the hairs on the back of his hand. Johnson was silent for a long time; then sighed and spoke:

"There is nothing, sir, too little for so little a creature as man. It is by studying little things that we attain the great art of having as little misery and as much happiness as possible."

The two walked on in silence, Boswell's face knotted with the labor of remembering.

Christopher smart knew a thing or two about insects but had no boxelder bugs with him in bedlam

Let Jether, the son of Gideon, rejoice with Ecchetoe which are
  musical grasshoppers.
For my seed shall worship the Lord as numerous and musical as the
  grasshoppers of Paradise.

Let Mizbar rejoice with the mayfly, as is their number
    so are their names, blessed be the Lord Jesus for them all.
For the names and numbers of animals are the names
    and numbers of the stars.

Let Pedaiah bless with the humble bee who loves
    himself in solitude and makes his honey alone.
Let Chalcol praise with the beetle, whose life is precious in the sight
    of God, though his appearance is against him.

*Let William rejoice with the boxelder bug, who goes about his
    business in silence, wanting only a quiet home by the coffee pot.
For in his nature he loves noise and size, and learns so little of
    himself, when the house fills up with his own trumpets ringing.*

BOXELDER GAVOTTE

Tempo di gavotte · strongly accented

Separate and mark

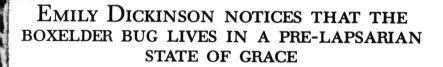

EMILY DICKINSON NOTICES THAT THE BOXELDER BUG LIVES IN A PRE-LAPSARIAN STATE OF GRACE

He does not bear — a heavy load —
Nor ever seem — to eat —
He knows not — labor — for his bread —
Nor longing — for his meat —

His pace is measured — as a clock —
He will not — hurry things —
His business — is — to carry calm —
And silence — in his wings —

THE HISTORY OF AMERICAN POETRY, OR: OSCAR WILLIAMS LOOKS AT A BOXELDER BUG FOR *READERS' DIGEST* BOOKS

1

I think I could turn and live with the boxelder bugs.
They are so placid and self-contained.
I stand and look at them long and long.
Boxelder bugs bring me tokens of myself.
I wonder where did they get those tokens?
Did I pass that way huge times ago,
and negligently drop them?

2

So much depends upon a boxelder bug
covered with soap suds beside the white sink.

3

Whose bugs these are I do not know.
His tree is in the village though.
He will not mind me stopping here —
To scoop up bugs before the snow.

4

I was of three minds like a window
In which three boxelder bugs are crawling.
A man and a woman are one.
A man and a woman and a boxelder bug are one.

5

The bug comes in on little bug feet
sits looking over stove and icebox
on silent haunches and then crawls on

I, too, dislike them; there are things that are important beyond
    boxelder bugs.
Killing them, however, with a perfect contempt for them, one
    discovers something like affection for the little bastards —
imaginary windows with real boxelder bugs in them.

Fat black bugs in a wine barrel room
Barrel house bugs with wings unstable
Sagged and reeled and expired on the the table
Boomlay, boomlay, boomlay, BOOM.

I thank you God for most this amazing
bug: for the crawling blackly spirits of trees
with a neat, sleek stripe of red, and for everything
which is unwanted, which is numerous, which is no.

I'd rather, except for the penalties, kill a man than a bug,
but the small black wing
had nothing left but a feeble wave which said, "Up yours."
I gave him the big thumb in the twilight

What happens to a bug in a window?
Does it dry up like a raisin in the sun
Or does it explode?
No. It eats in the kitchen and grows strong.

SHOULD YOU EVER FIND YOURSELF IN A CLASSROOM MANNED BY A PRACTITIONER OF THE HIDDEN MEANING SCHOOL OF LITERATURE, HERE IS AN EXAMINATION ANSWER STRAIGHT FROM THE BUG'S MANDIBLES

He is the fly on Buddha's nose,
the moon shadow falling
through your own curtain,
the leaping joy weighed down
with prayer books, balance sheets,
your mother's warnings still
crawling around on the edges
of your life to remind you.

72

Tom Guttormsson, who edits the *Minneota Mascot*, practices his literary criticism on boxelder bugs

I

They've been working for years
on a spray for boxelder bugs.
They should just forget about that
and use it on these poems.

II

I wonder
if boxelder
bugs can be
bored
to death

III

Two things in this world
you ought to accept peacefully:
dandelions and boxelder bugs.

THE WOMAN IN THE LIBRARY TELLS ME A DETAIL ABOUT BOXELDER BUGS THAT INTERESTS ME IN MORE WAYS THAN ONE

My boxelder bugs
wait for me
in the basement shower
every morning.
They get wet and
stick to you just
like that — all over.
I kind of like
it — actually.

When I mention the almost Lutheran cleanliness of boxelder bugs, a lady from Granite Falls speaks up firmly

They leave spots.
Curtains.
Doors.
Stoves.
Sheets.
Lightbulbs.
Bottles.
Me too.

And one lady comments:

Elms have got that Dutch disease;
Boxelders have got your poetry.

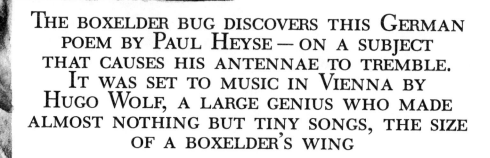

THE BOXELDER BUG DISCOVERS THIS GERMAN
POEM BY PAUL HEYSE — ON A SUBJECT
THAT CAUSES HIS ANTENNAE TO TREMBLE.
IT WAS SET TO MUSIC IN VIENNA BY
HUGO WOLF, A LARGE GENIUS WHO MADE
ALMOST NOTHING BUT TINY SONGS, THE SIZE
OF A BOXELDER'S WING

Auch Kleine Dinge: Even Little Things

Auch kleine Dinge können uns entzücken,
Auch kleine Dinge können teuer sein.
Bedenkt, wie gern wir uns mit Perlen schmücken,
Sie werden schwer bezahlt und sind nur klein.
Bedenkt, wie klein ist die Olivenfrucht,
Und wird um ihre Güte doch gesucht.
Denkt an die Rose nur, wie klein sie ist,
Und duftet doch so lieblich wie ihr wisst.

I — Translation

Even little things delight us;
For these little things we yearn.
Think how she is trimmed with pearls,
So dearly bought, so lightly worn.
Think how tiny the olive fruit is,
When you bite its succulence.
Consider how delicate that rose —
The sweetest breathing we can know.

II — Transcription

Feel the papery wings
tickle against your cheek
as they fly to bless a window
or swim through wine.
How even this tiny brushing
sends current through wires
running inside you if
you are still alive.

THE BOXELDER BUG LIVES INSIDE A STILL, ALIVE SILENCE YOUR OWN CIVILIZATION TOLD YOU FOR CENTURIES DID NOT EXIST. BUT IT DOES! HERE ARE TWO TRANSCRIPTIONS OF GOETHE'S POEM, FIRST IN WORDS, AND AFTERWARDS, IN A SETTING OF THE GERMAN BY FRANZ LISZT, TRANSCRIBED FOR THE LEFT HAND ALONE

Wanderers Nachtlied II

Über allen Gipfeln
Ist Ruh,
In allen Wipfeln
Spürest du
Kaum einen Hauch:
Die Vögelein schweigen im Walde.
Warte nur. Balde
Ruhest du auch.

— *Johann Wolfgang von Goethe*

Yellow Medicine River Nightsong

The beaver's tail slaps
nothing for a while;
a red hawk sleeps
alone on a post;
hear boxelder bugs breathe
in the dark grove;
just wait — soon this'll happen
inside you too.

a transcription for left hand alone of Liszt's setting of Goethe's poem

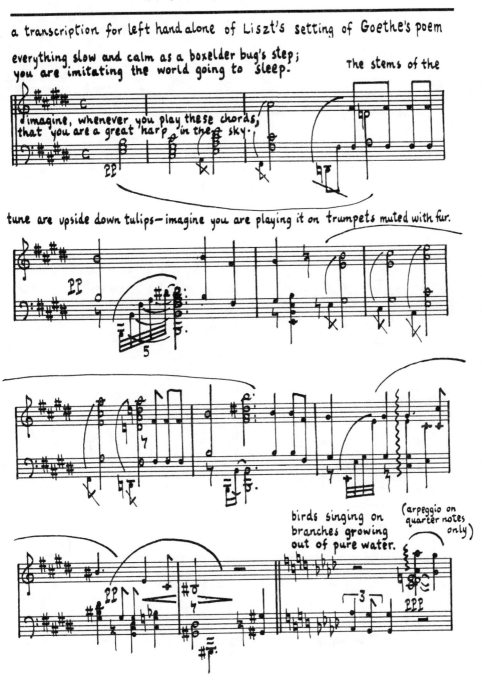

everything slow and calm as a boxelder bug's step;
you are imitating the world going to sleep.

The stems of the

imagine, whenever you play these chords,
that you are a great harp in the sky.

tune are upside down tulips—imagine you are playing it on trumpets muted with fur.

birds singing on
branches growing
out of pure water.

(arpeggio on
quarter notes
only)

Boxelder Bug Variations

imagine the noise of a lunar eclipse — take the time it takes snow to fill up the Grand Canyon.

now you will see that your right hand, if you have one, is doing something else, quietly.

Boxelder Bug Variations

Liszt's friend, the Hungarian count Geza Zíchy,
shot off his right arm while hunting. He was
not, so far as we know, hunting boxelder bugs.
Liszt made his only left hand transcription
for Zíchy, a choral piece of his own called
"Hungary's God." If Hungary, indeed, had
one, and He provided an afterlife (though
perhaps without Saint Paul's glorified body
which might have filled up Zíchy's empty
sleeve with an improved spiritual right arm),
here is another piece for Geza to practice.
Even if there is none, you may play it, too.

Afterword for the Player

While playing this piece with left hand alone,
you may keep your right hand in your pocket, or
    smoke,
blow your nose, turn pages, wave,
speak slowly to the deaf, or scratch your ear.
If, on the other hand, you worked around a baler,
or handled explosives carelessly, or fought
in any variety of American war,
you will probably not do anything
except play the piece with left hand alone.
Those who save half of what they own feel one pleasure;
those who spend everything they have feel another.
And who is to say which is the greatest pleasure?

THE ART AND SIGNIFICANCE OF TRANSCRIPTION CONSIDERED IN REGARD TO THE BOXELDER BUG WHO HAS TRANSCRIBED HIMSELF INTO YOUR CONSCIOUSNESS: A MEDITATION ON AN IDEA FROM FERRUCIO BUSONI

I

The frequent opposition aroused by my transcriptions and the opposition which senseless criticism often evoked in me made me try to reach some clarity on this point.

My final opinion about it is this: that notation is itself the transcription of an abstract idea.

The moment that the pen takes possession of it, the thought loses its original form. The intention of writing down an idea necessitates already a choice of time and key. Even if much of the idea is original and indestructible and continues to exist, this will be pressed down from the moment of decision. The idea becomes a sonata or a concerto; this is already an arrangement of the original. From this first transcription to the second is a comparatively short and unimportant step. Yet, in general, people make a fuss only about the second. In doing so they overlook the fact that a transcription does not destroy the original; so there can be no question of loss arising from it. The performance of a work is also a transcription, and this too — however free the performance may be — can never do away with the original. For the musical work of art exists

*whole and intact before it has sounded and after the sound is
finished.*

It is, at the same time, in and outside of Time.

— Ferrucio Busoni

If, as Busoni says, all notated music is transcription of an idea — an
arrangement of notes that moves faster in the mind than can be
caught by the transcribing hand — then all stories and images (which
professors call literature), are transcriptions of the movements of
boxelder bugs through the imagination. This, you might argue, is
unlikely, given the insignificant nature of the bug. He operates, you
say, under three disadvantages:

1. He is local — not known in London, Tokyo, or San Diego.
2. He is small — majesty is not commonly ascribed to him, as it is to
   the lion, elephant, or dictator.
3. He is silent — which is only another way of saying that we do not
   hear his singing.

Here are three analogies from music to counter this argument.

1. J.S. Bach: bodily the most local of men; his reputation was small
   and inaccurate; his own children mistrusted and rejected him. He
   was, on the other hand, likely the largest genius *of any kind* that
   has kept us company here on earth.
2. Anonymous: who thought so little of the majesty of his name that
   he did not bother to attach it to the million songs, dances,

catches, and hymns that are the spine of everything that lives in our throat and fingers.

3. Anton Bruckner: an Austrian of utterly conventional and sentimental mind; a man banal enough by appearances to make a boxelder bug comparatively resemble Lord Chesterfield, or La Rochefoucauld. He made what was inside him, including that smallness, into cathedrals of sound whose spires are beyond our sight. They break the heart with joyfulness.

And here are three analogies from literature:

1. Issa: half-starved, sunk in bad luck, he heard the Buddha singing in a frog croak. In hundreds of frog poems, he watched the universe by watching frogs closely. If Issa had known boxelder bugs, he would have admired and written lovingly about them. There was, for him, no such thing as a subject too small or insignificant to be appropriate for praise. When his infant daughter died, he made this small poem:

> The world of dew
> is a world of dew, and yet . . .
> and yet . . .

2. The anonymous Icelander who made sagas and imagined that stories about petty quarrels between small farmers on a bleak rock a thousand miles from any genuinely habitable place were of interest and deserved to be told beautifully. They have in them the grandeur of the inconsequential.

3. J.F. Powers: a Minnesota writer whose only material is the workaday lives of priests in rural Catholic parishes in the Midwest. This seems a subject of staggering smallness, but a Tibetan or Kunapipi reading Powers' stories would understand immediately that he described their inner lives accurately, and that the priestly paraphernalia was metaphor for yaks or boomerangs — or boxelder bugs.

One could as well make triumvirates of analogy from architecture, philosophy, cooking, or physics. The bug is a kind of quantum particle of the imagination — the irreducible matter that will not behave as it ought to, because your watching makes you author of its trajectory across the sunlit window.

II

Back to Busoni. His idea about transcription comes from an essay in which, defending Liszt against charges of being a charlatan and hack (in other words, a mere transcriber and thus corrupter of others' music), Busoni defends himself by appropriating all music, and, by analogy, all other arts under the umbrella of mental transcription. Busoni was too intelligent not to realize the outrageousness of this generalization. I agree with him.

Musical notes are nothing but a line of boxelder bugs crawling aimlessly through the imagination. A Bach grabs them, and arranges them on paper. Still they are silent as a Tabernacle Choir of bugs. But now they have been made to march in theoretical step, and can be given the gift of sound.

Have you a wood flute, hollowed out with a jackknife? Have you a kazoo? A violin? An empty wine jug? Then you have the *Art of Fugue* or *Don Giovanni* or "Gretchen am Spinnrade" or "Stormy Weather." You can give sound to music, clever human!

Liszt, as Busoni says, was one of the most remarkable givers of sound that the race has yet produced. He was all sponge; whatever came into his ear or across his eye came squiggling out from his piano. Nothing was too fantastic for him to make his own noises out of it: Palestrina motets, Bach fugues, Mozart operas, Beethoven symphonies, Schubert songs, the fiddle and hurdy-gurdy tunes of gypsies. Once music existed, the number of sounds it could assume was infinite, as the number of boxelder bugs, or as one boxelder bug.

Since Liszt was Liszt and not Reverend Peterson, Professor Tomthaus, or you, his own peculiar intelligence and character colors the sound of all that music. Playing his transcriptions gives you the possibility of lively conversation with an extraordinary man a hundred years dead. What did he think of Mozart? Play the *Don Juan Fantasy* and he will tell you. Some people capable of playing the transcriptions choose not to for reasons of taste and squeamishness. This is hard to understand. Who would live next door to an affable genius and not have coffee with him because he smoked cigars, or had a weakness for countesses? One is *not* so interested in what Liszt thought of Princess Wittgenstein as what he thought of the "Liebestod."

The material of any work of art — a chair, an afghan, an equestrian statue, a waltz — is so amorphous and mysterious that probably only a psychologist, an executioner, or a full professor would be fool enough to try to name it, or even describe it in its own language. An artist, on the other hand, gives it a body, and a body, since it exists, is true. A boxelder bug is as satisfactory a body as purple, or a saxophone, or French, or obsidian. Every artist makes some deformities, eyeless monsters imagined with good intentions and an imperfect hand. As in all species, these aberrations die young, before they reproduce. The strong and vigorous bodies — Homer, Leonardo da Vinci, Beethoven — eat, live to old age, and breed: never many, but enough, as there are always enough boxelder bugs in your line of vision to remind you that the planet is still safely turning in its own galaxy.

A BIRTHDAY FABLE FOR MY FRIEND ROLLIE JOHNSON, THE WOOD-CARVER, JANUARY 28, 1945–

A man sat whittling a cave one day, carefully hollowing a branch with his sharp knife. When he finished, he intended to crawl in, solve once and for all the mystery, the inner life of wood, the dancing inside the tree. After living in the dead tree heart for a while, he would know. This information, he thought, would help in thinking about human beings.

As his knife was about to penetrate into the unknown, he heard a small rustling sound like tiny wings shaking off wood dust. He peered inside the wood cave. A boxelder bug crawled slowly and calmly down toward the light. The carver put his ear close to the hollow wood and thought he heard words in something like English:

"I was napping, and heard scraping sounds. A minute ago I thought I smelled coffee. What year is this?"

"My God," the carver said, "How long have you been sleeping in this tree?"

"Dresden was burning, and a plane moved out over the water, something dark and heavy in its hold."

The carver put down his knife and thought: this is my life asleep inside this tree, and at the end of this cave, my death sleeps.

He stood up, brushing dust onto the rug, and put the almost hollowed branch into the fireplace. He began carving a woman's breast, and then an ear of corn, and then a wine bottle . . .

An unusual kind of love story, or perhaps, after all, usual

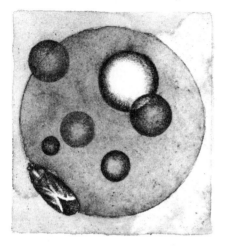

A boxelder bug fell in love with a human woman. One night while sleeping in a dresser drawer, he crawled inside the cup of a brassiere and was sure he smelled apples. How lovely to be a breast that smells like this, he thought, nestling his feet up into the indentation for the nipple. When daylight came, and she dressed, he watched her body stretch in the smoky light, heard the sound of water running, felt the vibration of shoes going down a long staircase, and knew she was gone out into the day.

He made his way over to the bed, finally reaching the pillow where her hair had slept. A few long strands of it lay there, black and silky. He rubbed his antennae against the whole length of a hair, sliding up and back as if crawling on a precarious rope bridge over a bottomless canyon, swaying and swaying. In fact, he had already fallen off this bridge, like a human being, into the gorge of love.

His whole body felt brisk, in a way it never had before. The air around his black wings was full of apples. He crawled to the mirror and began lifting wings and feet in a rhythm. Now his body did not seem so plain to him, not so much like other boxelder bugs. He had invented music and dancing in a single morning, and knew he would feel it forever.

The day passed slowly.

Just before dark, she came. He waited quietly by the side of an open book next to the bed, felt shoes drop on the floor, the swish of a blouse, her arm moving back and forth combing the black hair. During the course of the day, he had invented language and poetry together, and prepared rich moving things to whisper through his antennae into her ear. Naked now, she lit the lamp, the whole room drenched with the smell of apples, but now richer than apples, the smell of love, wind coming from so deep in the canyon that it had never been blown into the light before.

She began reading. He waited in the corner of the page, not daring to move, hoping she would mistake him for a word, or punctuation grown large, or a printer's error softened into an inky blur. His thin red stripes, his color, seemed terrible to him now, some shameful skulking nakedness. She read on, a sleepy smile coming up in the corners of her mouth, her eyes almost black.

HOW THEY DIE

They dry up,
turn into light.

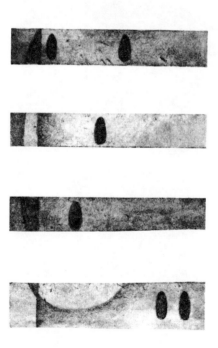

To Explain My Unusual Interest in Boxelder Bugs, Particularly Those Who Live in My Piano

I

I love whatever is difficult to kill:
Whales, grizzly bears, snapping turtles, boxelder bugs, some human
    beings,
Old Viking stories about corpses that won't stay dead.

I love stones that rest uneasy in the earth;
Boulders grunted up after the glacier;
Rock so anxious to see daylight, it bubbles out of volcano mouths.
I love water that freezes, takes a long time, and makes noises
Belching, snoring, moaning, sneezing, before spring melt.

I love old houses and barns that weather and lean into themselves.
You hear wind without opening the door.
The dresser leans forward.
Pictures slide to odd angles on the wall.
Weather comes, a guest, inside;
Still they refuse to fall unless
Beaten with crowbars and hammers.

II

You can kill anything by working at it;
The whole world of tame animals, dammed rivers,
Iron barns, tight houses, polished stones, helpful psychologists,
Heated pools, and half-dead people,
Wants you to join it,
Mails you invitations every day,
Each one more cordial and demanding.
Ignore them, and they grow hysterical, and will kill you.
Believe me, they can do it, and furthermore will be rewarded for it.
There is a bounty on *you*.

III

I was one hundred years old the day I was born, and knew all these
   things without words.
I felt it the first time I heard Beethoven played on a scratchy old
   record player.
I felt it the first time I opened my eyes at a funeral and saw that
   the corpse and I were the only two people alive in a full
   church.
I felt it at eleven years old when I bought Walt Whitman's poems for
   $3.50 in Sioux Falls.
I fingered the book for a long time, knowing inwardly someone had
   come close.
I feel it now, early in the morning the way the *Art of Fugue* moves
   around under my fingers on an old piano.

IV

Most of all, I love an old piano that refuses to die,
To be thrown in the chicken coop, chopped apart with an ax;
A patient piano that develops a sense of humor after sixty years,
A few water marks, a few scratches, a clatter in the bushings as felt
Hardens like an artery, a string going dead now and then.
This piano kept itself lean, doesn't eat much,
Its voice darkened and mellowed since 1922.
It plays noisy music quietly, quiet music like feathers dropped in a
   well.
It's fit for Bach now, and music by old men.
It likes human beings and is kind to them,
Doesn't even mind boxelder bugs that live in it.
This piano will die, too, but not before saving many times the odd
   man who plays it,
Sometimes gets out of bed late at night to feel its keys in the dark.

Boxelder Bug Variations

THOUGH WE FLATTER OURSELVES AS INDIVIDUALISTS, THERE IS ALWAYS ANOTHER PART THAT SUSPECTS THE CONTRARY TRUTH

I

All alike, they disappear
into each other's lives,
without detection;
one wing black as the other,
each stripe red as the next.
Death doesn't happen
bug by bug,
but by season.

II

With us it's different, we think,
each raised to be odd,
the center of his own world,
without which nothing else is;
and it all goes down
with a burst of weeping,
a hollow space in the air
where our body stood.

III

Sometimes I long
to disappear, be one
of millions wearing
the same wings, crawling
in the same window, sitting
in a room full of others,
invisible, have them wonder what
was his name? No matter. . . .

THE BUG LISTENS TO SLOW SAD BIRDSONGS IN THE AUTUMN MAPLE

Boxelder Bug Variations

Driving past Westerheim Graveyard
(Jonina Sigurborg Josephson Holm
June 23, 1910–May 25, 1975)

You must be dry as a spring boxelder bug by now
In your underground house;
Nothing but bones and a husk.
The rest stands, like the bug,
Next to the coffee pot
Ready to tell stories.

You always knew it would happen this way.
Even when you are not in a room, you are
In it, your voice everywhere,
Under cushions, back of the stove,
Coming out from mouths of painted figurines.
Your breath still blows dust around
Under bric-a-brac.
Eyes on the pictures blink.

Each fall, new bugs crawl in,
Make pests of themselves again
In the same old way.
They look just like last year's batch.
Maybe they are.
I don't have to tell you these things.

Thanks to:

The Bush Foundation for a grant which allowed the completion of what is perhaps the world's oddest literary project.

John Rezmerski for being a good friend and a brilliant editor. His help in encouraging, organizing, and weeding these bugs was incalculable.

The Music Department at Gustavus Adolphus College for having the courage and sense of humor to invite the first public performance of these bugs, both words and music, in October, 1983.

Kathleen and Lawrence Owen for feeding the maker of these bugs with affection, intelligence, and good dinners while he made them.

Charles Hamrum for the great gift of his wonderful interview.

Jim Phillips, composer and copyist, for bravely copying my bad musical hand.

Bill Holm was born in Minneota, Minnesota in 1943, the grandson of Icelandic immigrant farmers. He went to Gustavus Adolphus College and the University of Kansas. He taught literature and writing at Hampton Institute in Hampton, Virginia; Lakewood Community College in White Bear Lake, Minnesota; and at Southwest Minnesota State University in Marshall, Minnesota. He was a Fulbright lecturer in American Literature at the University of Iceland in Reykjavik and received a Bush Foundation Arts Fellowship in 1983. He is an enthusiastic musician and continues to live in a rickety old house in Minneota with boxelder bugs, several thousand books, and a couple of pianos, a harpsichord, and a clavichord, all of which he plays at odd hours of the night. His other works include *The Music of Failure* (Plains Press, 1985), *Coming Home Crazy: An Alphabet of China Essays* (Milkweed Editions, 1990), and *The Dead Get By with Everything* (Milkweed Editions, 1991).